May the peace of
God rest upon you.
Yvette

Copyright © 2019

All rights reserved. This book or any portion thereof may not be reproduced or used in any manner whatsoever without the express written permission of the author except for the use of brief quotations in a book review.

First Edition, 2019

Scriptures quoted from the King James Version of the Holy Bible.

~ Dedication ~

With a humble heart I offer thanks and praise to God, my Creator in Heaven, for making this opportunity possible. When I did not always understand the whys, it was your unmerited love and favor over my life that has kept me and continues to keep me, not only in the best of times, but also the worst of times.

It often takes the gentle push of others to help you get to where God wants you. Over the years, my mother was leading me down a path I never dreamed in a million years I would end up. Because she believed in me, this book is dedicated to the memory of my beautiful mother, Lottie. Although she is longer with me in the flesh, her spirit and legacy will forever live on in me.

To my husband, Alfred, thank you for always supporting and encouraging me in my endeavors. As we've walked hand in hand down through the years, I am thankful to God for everything He's done in our lives; for the things He is doing now; for everything He is preparing us for. Thank you for loving me and being my biggest supporter.

To my sons, Alfred Jr., Nicholas and Sentaura, although at times I've pushed you to excel, the reality is you pushed me to be the best mom I could be to you. Thank you for pushing me, believing in me and for being some of my biggest supporters.

~ Introduction ~

Sometimes in life, we hold on to past hurts and our perceived failures as if they were security blankets protecting us from disappointment. Holding on to past hurts does not protect us, it stifles our growth. It limits our ability to see with the eyes and the heart of God. It prevents us from following the quiet voice of God that whispers in our ears daily if we will only listen.

In my own life, God has shown me areas where I am holding on to past hurts. Getting to a place of totally letting go and turning it over to Him was difficult because in doing so, I had to deal with emotions, I otherwise would have just brushed off and not thought about them. In order for me to continue growing into the person He wants me to be, I had to deal with those emotions and allow Him to heal me.

As I began this journey, I developed a personal theme, "Trusting God". During this time, I've encountered many trials and tribulation but guess what? I am still trusting God. Even when the road has appeared hard, dark, lonely, unknown and dreary because I believe regardless of anything I've endured, my latter will be greater than my beginning.

Over the years, I've faced many trying times and my faith has been tested, but I had to learn to encourage myself in the Lord. 1 Samuel 30 records how David, though in the midst of turmoil and distress, strengthened himself in God. We must be intentional in encouraging ourselves because there is no situation too hard for God to handle. It is my prayer you will be encouraged and blessed by the words and pages in this devotional.

"the Lord answered me: "Write the vision, make it plain on tablets, so he may run who reads it."

(Habakkuk 2:2)

> *"But ye are a chosen generation, a royal priesthood, an holy nation, a peculiar people; that ye should shew forth the praises of him who hath called you out of darkness into his marvellous light;"*
>
> *1 Peter 2:9*

ঔঔঔঔঔঔঔঔঔঔঔ

Today is a good day not based on how you feel but because you are blessed to see it. And since this is the case, why not walk proudly as a whole woman equipped to do the work God has for you to do. It has been by no mistake that you are reading this message, for God had already predestined this to be.

Please know and beware, that there will come a time when you will be tried and tested because the enemy (the devil) wants to see you stumble and fall and become a stumbling block for others. But stay strengthened and know that even during those times you are knocked off balance, God is there, and He will not leave you nor forsake you.

Since you are a daughter of the King and whole woman equipped with the Word of God, you cannot be the same person you were before you accepted Christ as your personal Lord and Savior. You should be better! You have been given the tools to prepare you to be a better person. You should live in a way that people look and wonder, "What's gotten into her?" "She's not acting or talking like she used to." "Something's different about her." Be intentional to live your life in such a way that even if someone spoke badly about you, no one will believe a word said.

So, my dear sister in Christ, live with a determination to live your life as whole woman equipped by God, because after all, you are a kept woman with BUT God moments. And by that, I mean:

There have been times you thought you would lose your mind, BUT GOD kept you sane.

There may have been times when you thought you couldn't go on any longer, BUT GOD kept you moving.

You may have had times when you wanted to tell somebody off, BUT GOD kept your mouth shut.

You may have had time when you thought you would fall, BUT GOD kept you up.

You may have had times when you thought you were weak, BUT GOD kept you strong!

We can go on and on with your But God moments and how God has kept you, but this is just the beginning because as daughters of the King, you still have not seen your best days or greatest victories yet!! This is just the beginning to all God has in store for you!

You truly are blessed to be kept by the grace and love of God!

~ 2 ~

"Create in me a clean heart, O God; and renew a right spirit within me"

Psalm 51:10

൴൴൴൴൴൴൴൴൴൴൴

In Psalm 51:10, David prayed this prayer asking God to create in him a pure heart and renew the right spirit within him when confessed his sins to the Lord. Sin taints the heart. Even if you are tempted to say, "no one can see that, David didn't look any different after he sinned. But when your heart is corrupt, everything is corrupt. This is why Solomon reminds you in Proverbs 4:23 to keep your hearts with all diligence, for out of it springs the issues of life.

What happens when you turn on a faucet at home, and dirty water comes out? Chances are you will either contact a plumber or go to the hardware store, buy a brand-new faucet, install it and turn it on. Once you've gone through the necessary steps to replace the faucet, you turn it on and again, out comes dirty water. The problem was certainly not the faucet but the water source. So, it is with you. The heart is the center of your lives, and sin defiles it.

God can create a new heart and give a right spirit, not by your excuses but by your confession. You are all so prone to make excuses your sin. Yet, David confessed his sin, and God forgave him. God still disciplined David for his sin but He cleansed his heart, strengthened his spirit and created something new within.

What is your heart condition? Is it clean or dirty? Unconfessed sin in the heart contaminates the whole body. Never hold onto a sin or cover it; confess it immediately. When you do, God can cleanse and restore you.

~ 3 ~

Blessed is that servant, whom his lord when he cometh shall find so doing.

Luke 12:43

⚜⚜⚜⚜⚜⚜⚜⚜⚜⚜⚜

Do you sometimes suffer from the one-sided normal tendency to be ready soldiers only at certain times? Do you suffer to be a ready soldier only when you are riding the top of a spiritual or emotional experience? We should always be ready. Whether you feel like it or not! Whether it is popular or unpopular! Whether the crowd is with you or not! If you do only what you feel led to do only when things are going well, some of you would never do anything.

In Luke 12:43 you see that "if the master returns and finds that the servant has done a good job, there will be a reward." So, if there is a reward for the servant doing their job when the master returns, I ask these questions, what will my reward be? What will your reward be? Will you even get a reward? Please keep in mind that you should not work only to receive a material reward on earth, because they will pass away. However, you should be looking forward to the Ultimate

Reward and that is eternal life with Jesus, going back with Him when He comes!

The proof that your relationship is right with God is that you do your best for the Lord whether you feel inspired or not, and whether things are going well for you or not.

So, be ready, without worrying about who is here and who is not here because you are not working to please man, but you are working to please God. If you just do what God requires of you to do, He will do the adding and multiplying. Be ready doing what God wants you to do because you all will have to answer to God. And when you stand before God, will you hear him say, "Well done thy good and faithful servant" or "Depart from me"? What will God find you doing when He returns?

~ 4 ~

"Having a form of godliness, but denying the power thereof: from such turn away."

2 Timothy 3:5

✦✦✦✦✦✦✦✦✦✦✦

Walking down a dark alley, you notice a shadow. The closer you get, the larger the shadow appears to increase in size. But then you realize it's only a shadow, a silhouette. It's only an impersonation; it has no power, it is useless.

There are countless number of people daily professing to be children of God, but their lives speak something else. They have a form of godliness but deny the power thereof (2 Tim 3:5a). A form of godliness without real power is religion. Religion gives off the impression of something related to God. You can have the look and use the vocabulary and still be useless because you are missing God's power.

True godliness is a lifestyle that consistently reflect God's character. It is living everyday seeking ways to please God. It implies a real, personal relationship with God, always attentive to the presence and the power of God. Godliness is always associated with power!

If you are to bear the fruit of godliness, you must abide in Christ. Your roots must be deeply rooted Christ just as roots of a tree penetrate the soil. The saying goes "a tree is known by the fruit it bears." You have never heard of an apple tree bearing oranges or a pear tree bearing plums. The apple tree has a form of apple bearing that identifies it as such.

Every day God allows you to open your eyes, He is giving you one more chance activate the power of godliness. God is not mocked and cannot be fooled. Strive daily to live a life pleasing unto God, so in the end you will be able to hear Him say, "Well done"

~ 5 ~

Thou wilt keep him in perfect peace, whose mind is stayed on thee: because he trusteth in thee.

Isaiah 26:3

꧁꧁꧁꧁꧁꧁꧁꧁꧁꧁

Oh, my gosh! You have got to be kidding me. Did that really just happen? I must be on candid camera somewhere, I mean really! Has your mind ever been bombarded with these questions? How did you respond? Do you allow all the craziness and noise surrounding you to shift your focus or do you seek peace during the chaos?

There are times when you must take a step back in order to keep your focus on the One who brings peace. Your reactions to every situation presented to you daily can either make matters worse or better. Isaiah 26:3 reminds you that He will keep you in perfect peace if you keep your minds on Him.

That is not to say chaos and confusion will not come. But because He is not the author of confusion, it is not His desire for you to live in a chaotic world. <u>You cannot control what others around you do, but you can control how you respond.</u> Yes, you can have peace that surpasses all understanding when riding through craziness of this world when you make the effort to keep God at the fore front.

Think about it this way, will your getting upset and reacting negatively do anything to change the situation? If you are stuck in traffic, will your ranting and raving change the situation? If it's raining outside, will your fussing cause the rain to stop? Every day you are blessed to open your eyes, you decide how your day will go.

When you keep God at the table, even when trouble and chaos arise, He will prove himself to be Jehovah-Shalom. When it appears, the enemy has reared his ugly head to wreak havoc in your life, remember He is Jehovah-Nissi. No matter what's happening in you or around you, He is Jehovah Elohim.

The next time you find yourself facing a situation where you want to scream and maybe lash out, just look up and say, "Ok, God. It's in Your hands…what lesson are you teaching me today?"

~ 6 ~

"Whose adorning let it not be that outward adorning of plaiting the hair, and of wearing of gold, or of putting on of apparel"

1 Peter 3:3

֍֍֍֍֍֍֍֍֍֍֍

Take a mental journey with me if you will. Imagine walking into a room and seeing a beautiful fruit bowl filled with shiny red apples. They look so pretty and delicious. You pick one up to eat and just as you cut into it, up pops a worm. This apple, though shiny and red looking very delicious from the outside, yet, not worth eating.

We tend to dress up the outside to beautify our outward appearance. We adorn ourselves with the finest jewelry, nicest clothing only to realize on the inside you are carrying around dead bones. Bones depicted in the form of bitterness, unforgiveness, hatred, anger, jealousy, envy. And as you look a little closer, you see past hurts that you've not allowed yourselves to heal from.

You all have stood or may be presently standing in need of a spiritual cleansing – one that goes further than what is seen or heard by others. The cleaning that begins with the heart because it is your heart which flows the issues of life; then it flows into your minds, having renewed minds. No longer allowing garbage to take up residence in your mind but feed your mind the Word of God.

Just as David sought God and asked him to create in him a clean heart and renew the right spirit within him (Psalm 21:10), this should be our prayer daily. Every day you wake up, your minds need to be fixed and stayed on Jesus. It is when you keep your minds on Him that He keeps you in perfect peace (Isaiah 26:3).

By letting God work on you and clean you up from the inside out, you will begin to see yourself as the vibrant person God created you to be. Afterall, you are fearfully and wonderfully made. (Psalm 139:14)

"Cast thy burden upon the LORD, and he shall s[ustain thee: he] shall never suffer the righteous to be m[oved.]"

Psalm 55:22

ಞಞಞಞಞಞಞಞಞಞ

Have you ever felt like giving up? Have you felt as if the weight of the world was pressing you down? Do you feel as if you just can't take it anymore? You may even be saying, been there, done that, got the t-shirt.

Psalm 55:22a, tells you to cast your burdens upon the Lord and He shall sustain you.

This means when you are having these troubles you need to take them to God, give them to Him and He will carry the load.

What are you waiting on? Go ahead and give all your burdens and troubles to the Lord…ALL – not some. You may be thinking, well that is easier said than done. But is it? It is only as hard as you make it.

When you are facing pressures of life, instead of looking at what's going on around you, refocus and look at who is working IN you. Jesus will be your Problem Solver, if you will it to Him. He can't fix what is broken or messed up if you don't release it to Him.

From time to time, I'm sure you've been told that God won't put more you than you can bear. Just because you may feel like you can't take anymore, God knows you better than you know yourself and He really does know how much you can bear; after all, it was He who made you and not you ourselves.

Many times, when you are going through, it is because God wants to refine, reshape, remold you. He also wants to grow you up. For this process to take place, you must go through the fire. While in the fire, you must keep the faith and keep hoping and trusting because it will not last always.

Be encouraged as you continue on for the cause of Christ. Don't give in, don't give up, don't quit! Your trials do not come in life to tear you down, but they come to make you strong. You must keep trusting, keep believing and keep the faith because if you just hold out in God's own time, your change will come!

~ 8 ~

"According as his divine power hath given unto us all things that pertain unto life and godliness, through the knowledge of him that hath called us to glory and virtue"

2 Peter 1:3

ఈఈఈఈఈఈఈఈఈఈఈ

Where are you sitting? When the troubles of life are raging, when the storm winds blow, when life happens, where do you find yourself? Are you wallowing in a sea of self-pity, looking for every reason why you should just give up and throw in the towel? Or do you find yourself sitting at the feet of Jesus?

Everything you need, you can find at the feet of Jesus. When you are seated at His feet, you must use this as a time of pure and true worship; just as the woman with the alabaster box (Luke 7:36-50) was moved to who wash Jesus feet with her tears and dry them with her hair. She did this because she recognized Who He was. Once you understand Who He is in your life, you won't be able to just sit at His feet and remain emotionless. You won't be able to remain the same.

He knows each of you by name, He knows what you face daily, He knows every plot the enemy devise against you…when you are going through tough trials and tribulations,

He is there. When you are experiencing the highs and joys of life, He is there. Today and always, please remember, no matter where you find yourself in life, always stay at the feet of Jesus. He loves you even when you feel no one else does.

> "The LORD is nigh unto them that are of a broken heart; and saveth such as be of a contrite spirit."
>
> Psalm 34:18

༄༅༄༅༄༅༄༅༄༅

Yesterday it happened. For the first time in a few months, I can honestly say I felt better. I couldn't explain it even if I tried. However, all I can say is yesterday was a good day. Maybe it was the fact that I have slowly began getting back into my routine. Maybe it was because I've been reflecting on the good times I shared with my mom. Maybe it's because I've been thankful that my dad is still with you. Maybe it was because I got a chance to spend time with both my young men over the weekend. I don't know.

Even as I've been reflecting on memories of my mom. One story I shared with you continues to stick out and I believe that is my why. You may recall me sharing how mom chose to recite scripture when she came to a place of struggling to remember. That act alone has gotten me through these last few weeks. When I've found myself getting down, God's word has resonated in my head. Just as His Word kept my mom, it is keeping me. It is not to say I won't experience more days or moments of shedding tears because the physical me miss my mom, but, I must allow myself to have my moments and not let my moments have me.

Over the past few weeks/months, I've found great comfort in the word of God. Even during my moments of having a broken heart, God has been near. In fact, it has been during my pain that God has been closest to me. And the same holds true for you. Psalm 34:18 (NIV) reads "The Lord is close to the brokenhearted and saves those who are crushed in spirit." For the heart that is lonely, God gives a heart full of love. It is when you are at your weakest that God is your strength. When you are at your lowest, God gives hope to rise again. When you are at your saddest, God knits your hearts back together.

In those moments when you find yourself feeling down, instead of asking God "Why?", stop and ask "How?". God, how will I get through this? How will I laugh and experience joy again? And the answer is simply this: He hears you, and he cares for you. He is God and He can handle all your questions. God will meet you where you are. When your pain is the deepest, God remains with you. Isaiah 41:10 is a reminder that God is with you. He will strengthen, help and uphold you in His right hand. So, I encourage you today to step out in faith and seek God in your heartache and He will reveal His sovereignty.

~ 10 ~

"For I know the thoughts that I think toward you, saith the LORD, thoughts of peace, and not of evil, to give you an expected end."

Jeremiah 29:11

෴෴෴෴෴෴෴෴෴෴෴

Have you ever felt that God has packed up and moved and left no forwarding address? Do you ever feel that you are praying prayers that are going unanswered? Have you been praying for God to move in a situation or in someone's life and it seems that nothing has happened? How do you respond when God seems silent? Or could it be that God has given you the answer and you just don't hear Him?

First, you must realize that God is never silent. You are reassured in Psa. 139:7, 9-12 that you are not alone. Despite how you may be feeling, you are never out of God's sight. In those times you feel distant from God, you are probably the one who has moved so let's look to make sure you are walking in obedience to God. You need to also make sure in your praying that you are praying that God's will be done. Many times, those things you are praying are not what God has for you. So, it could be that He has answered that prayer and told you no or not now, but you are in denial. The only way to know this is to know His voice! It's is very important as children of God that you know His voice. You should learn how to listen for that still small voice. God knows the plans He has for you (Jere. 29:11) and you must also remember that His thoughts are not your thoughts neither are His ways your ways (Isa. 55:8).

Often when you are praying and asking God to fix a situation or person, what God really wants to do is work on you. In His working on you, He is preparing you for the work that will take place in that situation or person, so you will be ready for all that He is about to do.

Yes, you should always pray for others, but let's not forget you need to pray and ask God to continue to move and work in your lives and continue to mold and shape you into the person He wants you to be. God knows you better than you will ever know ourselves. You must trust and believe that He is there working on your behalf. It may not always be in the way you want or in a way that you understand, but all things do work together for good to those who love the Lord (Rom. 8:28) and even if you don't understand it now, you will understand it better by and by!

~ 11 ~

"These things I have spoken unto you, that in me ye might have peace. In the world ye shall have tribulation: but be of good cheer; I have overcome the world."

John 16:33

❧❧❧❧❧❧❧❧❧❧❧

With each season, we encounter, a change in the weather. We tend to watch the weather report, so we can be properly dressed. You don't want to leave home with shorts on and it's snowing outside. The way you dress when you leave home every morning, has a big impact on how your day will go. The same way, the way you dress spiritually plays a role in how you handle situations in your life.

Have you ever found yourself in a situation where you felt you were being attacked? Not necessarily a physical attack, but maybe a verbal attack? You know those moments when your flesh just wants to jump out and slap someone. Do you ever stop to think, "Now what would Jesus do in this situation?"

If you did ask yourself that question, you know exactly what Jesus would do. You can recite scriptures that tell what He did. Jesus was given the grace by the Spirit of God to complete all His assignments. As a Christian, you have the power to overcome any and all circumstances that come your way too.

Someone once said, "the higher the level, the stronger the attack." Meaning, the more you pursue God and do things according to His Word, the more the devil will come against you. The forces of evil will not take a back seat when you resolve in your heart to please God and follow after Him. It is almost as if you are waving a red cape in front of a bull, knowing this just makes the bull charge after you more mightily.

When you stand in the face of a testy situation, do you do what you know, or do you do what you feel? Can you hear that small voice say, "Don't panic, it's only a test you're going through." If it is only a test, you can pull out all your study material and focus on the Teacher and follow the leading of the Holy Spirit, or you could "just go there" and satisfy your immediate reaction to fight fire with fire.

As a Christian, your heart will not let you go there! And even if you do "go there", the Holy Spirit will convict you until you get it right. In your flesh, you may have wanted to tell someone off and stoop to their level to display ugliness. And it would have felt good – at the moment – but the consequences of doing things your way and not God's way, has a high price tag.

God's way is the high way! By humbling ourselves and walking the way Jesus did, you will be exalted. You will rise above the fiery darts. God will take the bad situation and work it for your good. You will gain respect and your enemies will leave scratching their heads because you have not responded the way they thought you should.

So, back to the opening statement: The way you dress when you leave home every morning, plays a big role in how you handle everyday situations in life. Is your hair fixed? Did you put on your helmet of salvation that guards your mind? Is your bra padded? Did you put on your breastplate of righteousness, which is your protective covering over your heart? Is your girdle/belt tightened? Did you put on and fasten your belt of truth in your heart and mind, so you won't sin against God? Did you put on your stomping shoes? Are your feet fitted with the readiness that comes from the gospel of peace? Since you are going to make sure to fix your hair, pad your bras, tighten your girdles and put on your stomping shoes, you can't afford to leave home without your coats – your shield that cover you and your swords that give you the truth to fight your enemies.

The next time you feel you are being squeezed, make sure you are properly dressed in the whole armor of God. Make sure your faith is solid, and your mind is made up to trust in the Lord with all your heart! Make sure your shields have been soaked in the powerful blood of the Lamb! Make sure you are determined to hold to God's unchanging hand and hold on to the sword of the Spirit (the Bible) as the unwavering truth that can give you all the fighting instructions you will need.

So, my dear sister in the Spirit – when the pressures of life seem to overtake you, don't give in, God wants you to win!!!!!

~ 12 ~

> "As it is written, I have made thee a father of many nations, before him whom he believed, even God, who quickeneth the dead, and calleth those things which be not as though they were."
>
> Romans 4:17

✥✥✥✥✥✥✥✥✥✥✥

When you are going through a difficult time in life, how do you deal with it? Do you crawl up in a corner and accept defeat or do you believe that although things look a little bad right now, they will not stay that way?

So many times, you do more harm than good by what you speak out of your mouths. If you constantly look at all the negative and never look for the positive, then you will always be defeated. The Word of God tells you that God desires that you speak those things that are not as though they were (Romans 4:17). You must also realize death and life lies in the power of the tongue (Proverbs 18:21).

When we speak words, we should look at things from fact and reality point of view in an effort to exercise our faith. The fact may be there is sickness in the body – but the reality in faith is by His stripes you are healed (Isaiah 53:5). The fact may be there is a lack of funds/food but the reality in faith is my

God shall supply all my need according to his riches in glory (Philippians 4:19). The fact may be there are enemies all around but the reality in faith is God will prepare a table for me in the presence of mine enemies (Psalm 23:5).

It is indeed a fact that you will all experience good days as well as bad days. What matters most is how you respond in those times you feel your backs are up against the wall. You never know how much influence you can have over others by the way you respond to various situations. I recall when my maternal grandmother became ill, we had to watch this strong woman of God go from being one of the healthiest people, to being confined to a wheel chair after suffering a stroke. She had to learn to walk, talk and write all over again. A few years after this, you were there again watching as she had to undergo surgery to have a blood clot removed from her brain. Our family was devastated because the doctors did not think she would pull through the surgery. But God had other plans! During this period, my grandmother was not looking at the facts as pointed out by man, but she was looking at the reality in faith that she would be healed and made whole, in the manner God saw fit for her healing to take place. Just looking at my grandmother, no one would have ever known all the things she endured in her life and that is because her focus was on God – not the problems.

I once heard a preacher say that often when you are going through situations in your life, your biggest mistake when you pray is asking God to give you a 360° turn from the situation. In doing this, you are turning around only to face the situation again. What you should do is ask God to give you a 180° turn. By doing this, your back now faces the situation. How many times have we asked God to turn a situation around? But it has not been to the point of taking our eyes off the situation. We must turn our backs on a problem to get our focus back on God. The devil wants nothing more than for you to stop seeking God and start looking at the situation. It is in those times that are most trying that you need to focus on God and not what it looks like on the outside.

Just because things look bad right now, know it will not stay that way. Instead of speaking negatively when situations arise, focus on the promises of God. Or just hit rewind in your mind and remember how God brought you out of another situation and believe if he did it before, he can do it again! As the songwriter says, "He brought me through this – He brought me through that – Lord I'm grateful to you!"

Walk in your victory! Know who you are! You are a child of the One who took the sting out of death! The battles you fight are not ours – they belong to God and once you take your hands off, He will bring it to pass. Even if it appears the devil might win the battle does not mean that he will win the war! You already have victory is in Jesus!

~ 13 ~

"Thou wilt keep him in perfect peace, whose mind is stayed on thee: because he trusteth in thee."

Isaiah 26:3

ઝઝઝઝઝઝઝઝઝઝઝ

So often you are asked the daily question, how are you doing? To which many of you reply, I am doing OK. However, if you stop to think about it, are you really doing OK or are you just pretending? After all, you can't let others know that you are having a bad day. What will they think? You have an image to up-hold and admitting that things are not going good right now will show others that you are human. Can you really stand to be that transparent?

I don't know about you but for me there are days I've woke up in some type of mood. I later came to realize it is during these times, I must continuously stay in contact with my Heavenly Father. This is when you must pray and ask Him to keep you in check; to give you a clean heart; to help you keep your mind stayed on Him. For the scripture tells you in Isaiah 26:3 that He will keep you in perfect peace, if you will keep your minds stayed on Him.

Now, don't get it twisted, I am not telling you to tell your personal business to everybody who asks how you are doing; some people cannot handle to hear what you have going on in life. But I do say, whatever you are going through, take it to God in prayer! He already knows what you are going through any way. Chances are, He will send the right person along who will be able to not only encourage you but to also pray with and for you.

You may even get to a place, where you must speak with God and God alone. No one else is around. Sitting in your car, at your desk…only speaking silently to God. People looking only see your lips moving but hear no sounds coming from your lips. They may even begin to wonder if you are crazy, but what they don't know is that you are pouring your heart out before the Lord. Let people watch, let them wonder, let them talk but just as it did not stop Hannah in 1 Samuel from speaking to God in her heart, don't let it stop you.

It really is ok to come clean and confess to God when you are having a bad day. You can simply make this your confession to God:

Lord, today is not a good day for me,
yet I am trusting that even as I go through this day,
You will do your God-thing and work everything out in the way you see fit for my life.
Lord, I know that even though, I am having a bad day,
I don't have to let my circumstances define me because I know who I am in You.
Neither do I have to let the fact that I am having a bad day cause me to forget regardless of the circumstances or situations,
this is still the day the God has made – I will, I shall, I must rejoice and be glad in it! In Jesus Name.
Amen.

~ 14 ~

"And David was greatly distressed; for the people spake of stoning him, because the soul of all the people was grieved, every man for his sons and for his daughters: but David encouraged himself in the LORD his God."

1 Samuel 30:6

֍֍֍֍֍֍֍֍֍֍֍

Both the hummingbird and the vulture fly over your nation's deserts. Vultures instinctively seek rotting flesh. They thrive on that diet. Hummingbirds ignore the smelly flesh, instead looking for the colorful blossoms of desert vegetation. The vultures live on remnants of a past life; they consume what is dead and gone. Hummingbirds feed on what is alive. They fill themselves with freshness and vitality. Each bird finds what it is looking for. Ultimately, you all do. Your attitude has everything to do with what you receive in life.

Attitude is simply your inward belief that causes an outward expression. Your attitude in turns determines your altitude. If you are experiencing all the highs and joys of life, you may find your altitude climbing, thus creating a great and pleasant attitude. However, if you find yourself facing tough times in life, your altitude may take a nose dive, which creates a nasty and negative attitude.

There are times when it seems everything that can go wrong in life, has gone wrong and just when you think nothing else can happen, the bottom falls out. During times like these, you must do like David in 1 Samuel 30:6, find your strength in the Lord your God. When you focus your eyes on God, your altitude begins to climb, and it shows outwardly in your attitude.

The next time you are facing moments where your altitude is taking a nose dive, be as the hummingbird and feed on what is alive; look for freshness and vitality and watch as your altitude begin to soar to higher heights. We serve a God who is greater than your circumstances and who deserves your praise no matter what you are dealing with in life. Make it your attitude to bless the Lord at all times and let His praise continually be in your mouth.

~ 15 ~

"For do I now persuade men, or God? or do I seek to please men? for if I yet pleased men, I should not be the servant of Christ."

Galatians 1:10

৯৯৯৯৯৯৯৯৯৯৯

Many times, you tend to let the thoughts and opinions of others get to you. You go about living a life to please others, to impress others, to have others like you. The Bible tells you that you should live to please God rather than man. It does not matter what you do, what you wear, or how you fix your hair. People will hate you just because you are who you are.

There comes a time in life when you must realize you are enough! Do not try to figure out why because some people will not like with without even knowing their reasoning. But don't use this as a time to hate them back – forgive, bless them and pray for them. Every person you meet in life was placed there for a reason. Some to bless you and others to test you. This may be the most important point. Whatever you do, don't allow the thoughts and opinions of others to cause you to not be the person God created you to be. Strive to be the best you God has created you to be.

What He has planted inside me, may not be the same as what He has planted inside you. However, when we take what has been planted within us, allow Him to water and care for it and we work together, uplifting and edifying His kingdom, we will see that it makes up a beautiful bouquet.

Remember even in a world that tells you, you are not enough, you have what it takes. Use your wits, do you and continue seeking to please God because you are enough!

Why am I confident in this? Because I know there is no greater strength than God's power within me. That same power is within you! The glorious power of God's love is what brings out the super possibilities us.

~ 16 ~

"So God created man in his own image, in the image of God created he him; male and female created he them."

Genesis 1:27

ঔ-ঔ-ঔ-ঔ-ঔ-ঔ-ঔ-ঔ-ঔ-ঔ

Many times, we pray and ask God to use us for His service, but we have not given ourselves totally to God, so He can use us. We hold on to past hurt and pain, we hold on to unforgiveness. Then we justify it by saying, "Lord, you just don't know how bad they hurt me." Forgetting this one fact: God created you. He knows all about you. He knows you better than you know yourself. More importantly, He knows the end of your life story, you don't.

Don't allow issues in life to alter or deter you from being who God has created you to be. We all have issues, but we also have a God who can handle any issue, if you will just allow Him.

As children of God, you should never feel that God does not know what you are going through. There is nothing in life that God cannot handle and bring you through. Whatever it may be, sincerely take it to the Lord in prayer and leave it there.

Easier said than done, right? Wrong! It's only as hard as you make it!

God wants all of you! Who are you to withhold any part of you from the One who created all of you in His very image? Ask God to show you who you really are and when He does, ask Him to mold you into the person He wants you to be. You all have areas in your live you need to work on, so don't concern yourself with others but pray that God will move in their life as He continues to move in your life.

God will not force Himself on anyone but when you sit and look at the ultimate sacrifice made for you, while you were yet sinners, why would you not want to give yourself to God? God sent His Son to die on the cross for you and me. He loved you before you were even formed in your mother's womb. He loved you before you took your first breath. Even when you went against His teaching and will for your life, He still loved you!

Go ahead, trust God to remove all those things you are holding on to. You know those things nobody knows about but you and God. Those things hindering you from giving your all back to God! If God truly is your all in all; your everything; the air you breathe; you should have no problem releasing your hurts, pains or your SELF back to Him! Give yourself away so

God can use you! God wants to do a new thing in your life – are you ready?

~ 17 ~

"The grass withereth, the flower fadeth: but the word of our God shall stand forever."

Isaiah 40:8

๑๑๑๑๑๑๑๑๑๑๑

Reflecting over the years, there have been seasons we have experienced trying and difficult times in my family. It would appear to many our faith has been tested more than once. Some of the trials and tribulations we've encountered left us somedays in places of almost giving up and walking away from all those things we knew God would wanted us to do.

For each person living, life hold many uncertainties, but there is one thing for certain. The Word of God. His Word will never falter nor fail. It has been His Word that kept and sustained us during these tumultuous times. And His Word has also and sustained you. Yes, in the flesh we may still hurt and grieve yet in the spirit, when we are weak, He makes us strong. Yes, in the flesh we want to give up and just say no more; yet in the spirit, we must press toward the mark for the prize of the high calling in God.

As I just stated, because of the things we endured, our faith may have been tested, but guess what, we did not give up.

You should not give up. Regardless what you may be facing, now is not the time to quit. Now is not the time to give up. There is someone who needs what God has deposited in you. We will all, at some point, face discouraging moments. We will all endure heartaches and pains. Yet, we shall remain confident in knowing greater is He who is in us than he who is in the world. You can overcome every obstacle, every heartache, every setback that comes your way. There is no situation you face that you cannot overcome. Jesus overcame and because He overcame, so can you. Since God wants to perfect the work He has begun in you, giving up is not an option. Keep pressing on!

When storms arise in your life, when times get hard, when you want to give up and quit, remember the last storm God brought you through. Quiet the voices in your head saying, "but you just don't understand, you just don't know what I am going through." Keep moving forward! Don't stop in the middle of the storm, hoping it will soon pass. Your stopping may cause the storm to last longer than God intended. Keep pressing on. Turn on your wipers. Praise your way out of the storm! Pray your way through the storm! Whatever it takes to get through the storm, just do it!

~ 18 ~

"For we are his workmanship, created in Christ Jesus unto good works, which God hath before ordained that we should walk in them."

Ephesians 2:10

⚜⚜⚜⚜⚜⚜⚜⚜⚜⚜⚜

As women of God, we have been called out as God's workmanship, created in Christ Jesus to do good works, which God prepared in advance for you to do. We are in the world but should not be of the world. God has called us not that we would conform to the world but be transformed by the renewing of our minds. We have been called to live holy and acceptable lives. Are you living up to this call God has placed on you?

We have been called out by God to lead by example. We can't talk one thing and walk another. We must make sure our walk lines up with our talk and more importantly our walk lines up with the Word of God. Galatians 6:7 states, "Be not deceived; God is not mocked: for whatsoever a man soweth, that shall he also reap." You may think you are getting away with living a double life. You may not reap what you've sown in this life, but future generations will. Rest assured one day you will stand before God and He knows all, sees all and will separate all accordingly. Those times you think no one else knows or sees what you are doing, remember God has an all-seeing eye.

We are called by God to walk the narrow way with Him. We should not be going the same way as the world. We read in Matthew 7:13-15, we should enter through the narrow gate. Wide is the gate and broad is the road that leads to destruction and many enter through it, but small is the gate and narrow the road that leads to life and only a few find it. Let you be among the few that travel the narrow road.

You must understand for you to be the woman God has called you to be, there are some changes that must be made. You cannot focus on what someone else is or is not doing, but you need to make sure you are doing what God wants you to do. You have been given an assignment to do from God. God has special plans for your life, plans to bless and prosper you but for you to receive the benefits of His plans, you must be willing to search for him, seeking him with all your heart so you will find Him. In being the woman God has called you to be, it goes beyond what you do. It's who you are. You are a chosen people, a royal priesthood, a holy nation belonging to God.

Decide today to make a conscience decision to make a change in your life. In making this change for the better, you need to start with the woman in the mirror and ask God to help you change your ways. You can be the person God has created you to be if you would humble yourself, pray, seek God's face, and turn from your wicked ways.

It is time to wake up, stand up and step up to be the woman God has called you to be.

~ 19 ~

"If the Son therefore shall make you free, ye shall be free indeed."

John 8:36

❦❦❦❦❦❦❦❦❦❦

Imagine you have been living for years captive. The enemy has you locked up in prison and there are chains on your hands and legs. Well, one day, someone walks in, unlocks your prison cell and unlocks the chains. What do you do? Do you leave out of the cell or do you stay? Do you put the chains back on and lock yourself back into the cell? If the opportunity presented itself to you to be set free, you would take it, right?

God sent His Son to die on the cross for you. When Jesus died on the cross, He took the sting out of death and the devil was defeated. Yet many refuse to take the chains that have them bound off. Why do you continue to keep the chains of bondage on, even after Jesus has declared you are free? You are the ones who keep putting them back on and the devil is sitting there laughing about it.

One thing the Holy Spirit revealed to me was how we often keep ourselves in bondage when we refuse to talk about that very thing God has delivered you from. Maybe you feel no one will understand what you've gone through. Maybe you feel others will look differently at you. Maybe you are afraid to talk about the thing God brought you out of…but remember God has not given you a spirit of fear.

Pray and ask God to reveal to you who you need to share your testimony with because just as sure as you are alive, there is someone out there struggling with the very thing God just delivered you from. Once you open up and share how God has brought you through that thing you have wrestled and struggled with for so long, you are willingly removing those chains. God will not force you to do anything – but He will be there to see you all the way through.

So what, if people don't understand you or don't want to hear you. So what, if people talk about what God has done in your life. Is it really that significant to you what others think? You will never be able to please everybody on this earth so get over it, get over yourself, and realize God has done a marvelous work in your life. Now why don't you run and tell that? Share it. Don't keep yourself locked up in bondage when God has already set you free.

I pray for whomever is voluntarily keeping themselves bond by these chains that you will allow God through the Holy Spirit to release those things! Do you believe that God wants you to be whole again? Release it, let it go! Do you believe that God wants what is best for you? Release it, let it go! Then you boldly declare:

I'm free, praise the Lord, I'm free.

No longer bound, no more chains holding me.

My soul is resting; it's just a blessing,

Praise the Lord, Hallelujah, I'm free!

~ 20 ~

"For the LORD your God is he that goeth with you, to fight for you against your enemies, to save you."

Deuteronomy 20:4

ఈఈఈఈఈఈఈఈఈఈఈ

Strike One. Strike Two. Strike Three. You're out. This is a common path of a baseball player when the pitcher throws a mean fastball, breaking ball or changeup. The batter often focusing hard on the ball, often misses the mark. And once again, goes back to the dugout with another strike out. Up comes a new batter. Ready to knock the ball out the park, then enters the pitcher. The devil. Satan. He pitches the first ball, it's a slider. Strike One. Next, he pitches a curve ball. Strike Two. Now he prepares to pitch a fastball, right down the middle in an effort to make you think you are about to get that home run. You swing just in time, only to here "Ball!" The devil prepares now to pitch what he knows will be the one to strike you out. But the coach calls a time out, and all of a sudden, there is a change up in batters. Jesus steps in, right on time as a pinch hitter.

The devil thought he defeated Jesus when He was on the cross. Strike One. Death thought it had defeated Jesus in the grave. Strike two. Oh, death where is your sting, oh grave where is your victory? The winning run was when Jesus rose from the grave. Because of this, you have total Victory in Jesus! What the devil has been doing to mean for bad, God has been working on your behalf. Not only is Jesus sitting at the right hand of God making intercession for you, He is also pleading your case to God. You have the best lawyer money cannot buy. Every problem you face is a case for Jesus to present to God on your behalf. Satan has no victory! He is so busy trying to do what he can to make you lose your joy, hope, trust and faith, even your mind. Satan does this because he knows his time is not long.

Just because you may have suffered or maybe suffering trials rejoice in knowing that God is preparing you for something greater! Just as God prepared the big fish to swallow Jonah – God is preparing something for you! You may not know it is He is preparing you for, but know you are in His hands and because you are in His hands, the devil cannot pluck you out.

You belong to the Most High God. Often when we are facing difficulties, we don't always want to hear he church clichés. You read your bible, you spend time in prayer with God. You know what the Bible tells you. You God is your Provider, God is your Way, God is your Bridge over Troubled Waters, just to name a few. Yet sometimes, we all need reminded that even when it looks like the fire will consume you, there is One more in the fire standing with you. Waiting and watching to see how you will respond. Will you continue to praise Him? Will you continue to read His word? Will you continue to trust Him? Do you really believe that even if He does not deliver you out of the fire that He is still able? Or will you just tuck tail, run and hide?

God knew these days were coming before they ever got here – remember, He created you, and he knew your end before your beginning. The trials and tribulations come as no surprise to God. He already knew and knows how this chapter of your life will play out. The key is, you must keep trusting and believing God has everything His hands. Yes, you may get weary, but you must get your strength from God.

When you come through your trying time, you will be able to look back and see God was with you the entire time. You will be stronger, wiser and so much better.

~ 21 ~

"Wherefore seeing we also are compassed about with so great a cloud of witnesses, let us lay aside every weight, and the sin which doth so easily beset us, and let us run with patience the race that is set before us"

Hebrews 12:1

૭૭૭૭૭૭૭૭૭૭૭

I'm not sure about any of you, but on occasion, I've found myself to be a part of this elite group known for carrying all the grocery bags in the house at one time. If there are several bags, I always think about how easily I can lift at least half, if not all those bags to save time and trips going back and forth. However, it's only when I get the bags loaded and begin the journey into the house that I begin to think, that was probably not a good idea. Often, the bags are so heavy they feel as if they are cutting into my skin or by the time I place the bags on the counter, it's extremely hard for me to lift my arm – but somehow, I manage. Once I put the bags down and I'm no longer carrying that weight, I feel relieved.

Such is the case in your Christian walk. Hebrews 12:1 state, "Wherefore seeing you also are compassed about with so great a cloud of witnesses, let you lay aside every weight, and the sin which doth so easily beset you and let you run with patience the race that is set before you." There is a race set before you to run but you can't run it carrying dead weight. There is a place God wants to take you spiritually and you are trying to include people and things on the journey who aren't meant to go with you. In order to run this race, you must understand there is a purpose and a plan for the race you are running and whatever your race will not be the same as someone else's. Focus on the race set before you.

I'm sure if you ask any runner, they will agree it's hard to run a race carrying weights. After a while, the weights will become too heavy for the runner to carry. Don't allow the cares of this world to overwhelm you or cause you to lose your focus. Don't allow the troubles of this world to cause you to carry weight that God never intended you to bear. You will endure moments when the weight of the world feels as if it is upon your shoulders, but you must remember to cast all your cares upon Him. His yoke is easy, and his burdens are light. Trust God no matter what you are going through; He will give you the strength you need to get through whatever situation you may be facing.

Put the weight(s) down. Let go of anything that may be weighing you down. Run your race and run it well, being content knowing the race is not given to the swift nor the strong but the one who endures until the end.

~ 22 ~

"Commit to the LORD whatever you do, and your plans will succeed. In his heart a man plans his course, but the LORD determines his steps."

Proverbs 16:3, 9

ꕥꕥꕥꕥꕥꕥꕥꕥꕥꕥꕥ

The best gift anyone can give a person who loves to plan is a monthly planner. A planner is that person always thinking ahead; being prepared; appearing to always be ahead of the game. However, as much as they love receiving those monthly planners, there are may be some things that are just beyond planning. As life doesn't always turn out as planned.

You don't plan for a broken heart. You don't plan for a failed marriage. You don't plan for to be laid off work. You don't plan to live paycheck to paycheck. You don't plan for an illness. You plan to be young forever.

You plan to climb the corporate ladder. You plan to be rich and powerful. You plan to be successful. You plan to conquer the universe. You plan to fall in love - and be loved forever.

You don't plan to be sad. You don't plan to be hurt. You don't plan to be broke. You don't plan to be betrayed. You don't plan to be alone in this world. You don't plan to be shattered. You plan to be happy.

Some people tend to think if they work hard enough, they can get whatever they want, and that may be the case. But in reality, most times, what you want and what you get are two different things.

You, being mortal beings, plan. But so does God in the heavens. God knows the plans He has for your lives. Your thinking is not like His thinking! There are times when it appears difficult to understand God's plans, especially when His plans are not what you thought they should be. You all have your own cross to carry, and none of you can choose the cross that God wishes you to carry. But you can carry your cross with courage, all the while knowing that God is always right there with you and will always give you strength you need to make it through any situation, crisis or trial that comes your way.

As you prepare for another new day, make your plans, but remember and understand that you live by God's grace and He has the final say. There is nothing in your life that you endure that God will not give you grace to endure for His grace is enough. Even at times, when things don't go according to your plans, remember God has a Master Plan.

~ 23 ~

"Let us break their bands asunder, and cast away their cords from us."

Psalm 2:3

ง็-ง็-ง็-ง็-ง็-ง็-ง็-ง็-ง็-ง็-ง็

Have you ever watched a dog on a chain? Noticing how hard he tries to go a little farther, but the chain always stops him at the same place, never letting him go farther and experience more? Even when people take their dogs on a walk, they leash them in an effort to keep the dog from going anywhere other than where the owner wants the dog to go.

Unfortunately, in many churches today, people are chained and remain in the same place. Rather than moving forward into what God wants to do in their lives, they remain in the same place where things are familiar, even if it is uncomfortable. As if they are on leashes preventing them from experiencing more than what the ruler of their lives wants them to experience.

There are many chains that you tend to struggle with today. These chains can be anything holding you back or anything that takes the life out of you, like chains wrapped around your neck. But you must continue to hang in there. Those chains have been broken. When you get to your breaking point and feel you can't go any further; remember if you cry out to God, and ask anything in His name, believing that it will be done. Those chains can be broken. It does not matter what you go through in life, God is bigger than every problem and He has all power to break every chain. There is power in the name of Jesus to break every chain. Focus on the word every. This tell me we cannot turn around and say, "well Lord, maybe You can break this chain, but I've been this way for a few years. This is who I am, I've tried to change many times, but nothing works." You must get out of your way, step out on faith, and believe God has more for your life than what you are experiencing.

There is indeed power in the name of Jesus to break every chain. You have the authority to proclaim that every chain in your life be broken in Jesus' name. You don't have to live bound anymore. God's already broken those chains. Freedom is ours. Chains can be and are already broken. You just have to step out of the shackles and into the freedom He has set before you.

What are you waiting for? Are you willing to let Christ break your chains?

~ 24 ~

Every branch in me that beareth not fruit he taketh away: and every branch that beareth fruit, he purgeth it, that it may bring forth more fruit.

John 15:2

ത്തെത്തെത്തെത്തെത്തെ

Pruning is an essential gardening skill. When you prune correctly, you encourage healthy growth and flowering, as well as good looks. Such holds true of us. No one likes the process of pruning and the pain of loss, but fruit only grow on new branches.

Pruning doesn't just mean spiritual surgery to remove what is bad. It can also mean cutting away what is good and better so that you may receive what is best. God often uses the shears of your circumstances, tough times, heartache, difficulty, physical ailments to prune you. Although you may not realize it, He is trimming off the roots that are not bearing fruit. "He cuts off every branch of mine that doesn't produce fruit, and he prunes the branches that do bear fruit, so they will produce even more." (John 15:2)

When you read and hear the Word of God you may get convicted. That is God cutting away the bad, so it doesn't get in the way of the good. Pruning can be painful, it can hurt, and it can cut. Yet, God prunes you because you are important and wants you to be fruitful. Oh, how freeing it is to get rid of the unnecessary! You must go through the process to progress.

Pruning is a necessary part of life; in order to move forward, you must let go.

~ 25 ~

"And Ruth said, Intreat me not to leave thee, or to return from following after thee: for whither thou goest, I will go; and where thou lodgest, I will lodge: thy people shall be my people, and thy God my God"

Ruth 1:16

❖❖❖❖❖❖❖❖❖❖❖

Regardless of what Naomi said to Ruth, Ruth was determined to leave all she had; she was determined to leave her former life behind.

There are things in our lives God has told you to leave behind in order to move on to the next level in Him. Do you have the mentality of Naomi? Will God have to get your attention and deal with you in a trying way? Do you have the attitude of Orpah? Can you truly find it in your heart to forsake the world and not turn back? Do you have the determination of Ruth? Determination to walk through the door of commitment in faith knowing that God has everything in control.

Why will you keep praying for God to change a situation if you will not accept the answer He has given you? Why will you keep praying and asking God to move a mountain, when you are doing everything you can to hold on to it? Why will you ask God to give you the strength the climb your mountain, when you don't want to put forth the effort to go when He say go?

In this life, you have so many people who refuse to totally be free. You attend various Women's Conferences/Workshops, worship services, revivals, prayer breakfast, yet you are still refusing to leave some other things behind. God has removed the shackles that have you bound, but there are so many, who willingly pick the shackles back up and put them back on. And according to John 8:36, "If the Son sets you free, you will be free indeed!" There are no more shackles on your feet, shackles on your hands…You are free!!! The only thing keeping you from having this freedom is your own selves.

Naomi had a choice. Orpah had a choice. Ruth had a choice. Today, you have a choice. God will not force anyone to do anything. You should follow God because you want to and not because you are forced to do so. You can choose to give it up, turn it loose, and move on in the Lord, or you can keep holding on to the thing or things that keep hindering you from being who God wants you to be.

Is the thing or things you are holding on to worth dying and going to hell over? What are you willing to forsake?

~ 26 ~

"And David was greatly distressed; for the people spake of stoning him, because the soul of all the people was grieved, every man for his sons and for his daughters: but David encouraged himself in the LORD his God."

1 Samuel 30:6

⫷⫷⫷⫷⫷⫷⫷⫷⫷⫷⫷

You are known by many as always having an encouraging word for someone. You always want everyone to see the class as half full and not half empty. But what do you do when you've poured everything you have into others and now you only see your glass and half empty? Those times when you don't feel like being an encourager. You always lend an encouraging word to others, but right now you are the one hurting. You have to pretend that everything is ok, when in fact, it is not. You have to walk around with a smile on your face, when what you really want to do is yell, scream, cry and/or hit something. How do you muenster up the strength to forge ahead? What do you do? Where do you turn? Who is there to encourage you?

The same way you have encouraged everyone else, you must also take time to encourage yourself in the Lord. Hit the rewind button in your mind and playback some of those same words of encouragement you've share with others. God has promised to keep you in perfect peace, if you keep your mind stayed on Him. Even when things are in disarray in your life, there is peace in Him. You know there is nothing that comes up in life that takes God by surprise. It may take us by surprise, but not God.

When you don't understand how what He is doing is for your good, you still have to trust that He knows what He is doing. When it seems hard and seems no one understands what you are going through. When you have done your best to do everything you think you are supposed to do, and even still, it is not good enough. God knows, and He cares. Even while you feel all alone, God is there; He will never leave you nor forsake you. Through it all God is still God.

Whatever you may be dealing with, turn it over to God. Yes, it is much easier said than done, but you must remember that God can do much more with any situation than you ever could. Even when it seems like all hope is gone. As you are struggling with the situation, the circumstance, the condition, the problem, I dare you to trust God! He really does have your best interest in mind because He already knows the plans He has for your life. We all will eventually go through the fire and right now, just may be the time He is purging you in the fire.

But when you come forth, you will be as pure gold. Maybe, right now is the time that He has placed you back on the wheel to mold and make you over into who He wants you to be. He wants to perfect what He started in you. He has more work for you. More people for you to encourage.

"But Lord, it hurts. Lord, when will the crying stop? Lord, when will the pain go away? Lord, when will it be over?" This season, this pain, this struggle you are in is only for a little while, for in due season you shall reap, if you faint not. Many times, you don't have to wait until you come through for God's deliverance, He can deliver you even while you are amid going through. Wait on the Lord and be of good courage. If you wait on the Lord, He shall renew your strength, you shall mount up with wings as eagles, you shall run and not be weary and you shall walk and not faint.

Dear sister, encourage yourself in the Lord for it shall come to pass that you will be strengthened in the Lord.

~ 27 ~

"A word fitly spoken is like apples of gold in pictures of silver."

Proverbs 25:11

֎֎֎֎֎֎֎֎֎֎֎

"Sticks and stones may break my bones, but words will never hurt me." How many times can you recall hearing or reciting this phrase? Do you believe this to really be a true statement? According to Proverbs 18:21, the power of death and life are in the tongue. So, what are you speaking into your life or the life of others? Death or Life?

Have you noticed how all it takes to put a smile on the face of someone who is going through a difficult time, or having a bad day, is a kind word? And at the same time, the words you speak can cause a person to feel as if their heart is breaking in two or cause tears, hurtful tears, to form in the eyes.

Words do have the capability of hurting, killing and cursing BUT if used correctly, and by the guidance of the Holy Spirit, your words can have the power to deliver, heal and bless.

You never know what battle someone else may be fighting and the very words you speak into the life of that person may be the words to help them heal and be delivered or can cause them to hurt worse. Never think the words that come out of your mouth are just "empty" words with no meaning. For somebody, your words will aid in that person deciding how their day will go. Luke 6:45 tells you that out of the abundance of the heart the mouth speaks. Each negative word you speak can give way to make room for more negative words. Reckless words are not under the guidance of the Holy Spirit and can lead to mistakes and unkind ways.

Each day you are blessed to open your eyes, remember that the very words you speak can build up or tear down. And since you profess to be Christians, you should want to speak words that encourage and build one another up.

It's time to take an inventory on the words you speak. This not only applies to people you encounter daily but take an inventory on the words you speak into your own life. If after taking inventory, you see a change needs to take place, pray and ask God to help you. Will you resort to being Negative Nancy or Negative Ned or will you decide today is the day you will be Positive Polly or Positive Paul? Choose to speak life and not death

~ 28 ~

"Set your affection on things above, not on things on the earth."

Colossians 3:2

☙☙☙☙☙☙☙☙☙☙☙

Life sometime have a way of bringing disappointments, setbacks, heartaches, and betrayals. Life also brings you many joys and mountaintop experiences. It's all about how you tend to view your situation and what you focus on the most.

You can decide to focus on all the bad things going on around you, celebrate those things with a daily pity party OR you can decide that no matter what is going on in life, today is the day the Lord has made, and I will rejoice and be glad in it.

No one is exempt from going through difficult times in life, but the key is not letting those difficult times to cause you to lose your focus. Keep your eyes on the ONE who can deliver you. Look to the ONE who can strengthen you.

Life – and the people in it – will never be perfect. This is earth. It can never be for you what only Heaven can. So, relax. Let it be what it is. Let them be who they are. And remember that the longing inside of you is because "He set eternity in your hearts." (Eccl. 3:11)

~ 29 ~

"To everything there is a season, and a time to every purpose under the heaven"

Ecclesiastes 3:1

❧❧❧❧❧❧❧❧❧❧❧

Past is defined in Webster's Dictionary as just gone, taken place in a period before the present. Future is defined as: that is to be.

Often times you sit and look back over your life and the things you did or did not do in life and sometimes find ourselves saying, "if only I had." We often spend too much time focusing on what we, ourselves, or someone else has done until you fail to see the future God has for you. You even miss out on how God has changed a person for His purpose and for His glory.

You cannot go back in time and change the things you have done. It is important to let go of the things that happened in the past and move on. Genesis 19 record the story of Lot's wife. She was turned into a pillar of salt because she did not want to let go of the past. She chose to look back in the past life, instead of trusting God with the future. Will you keep holding on to the past, or will you let it go and let God?

In Philippians 3:13, Paul tells you that you should forget those things which are behind you and reach forth to those things which are before you. When you focus on those things which are before you then you can have a peace that passeth all understanding, you can have joy that flows like a river, you can have love that runs from heart to heart.

Let's face it, everyone has a past, whether it be good or bad. But will you let your past determine the future God has for you? You all have a choice...a choice to keep living in the past or a choice to press toward the mark for the prize of the high calling of God which is Christ Jesus.

2 Corinthians 5:17 tells you that you are new creatures in Christ, all your old things are passed away. This means, you have to let go of the past because you are now like new.

Although you cannot alter your past, with God, you can determine your future.

Romans 8:28 you are told that all things work together for good to them who love the Lord.

Philippians 4:13 you are told that you can do all things through Christ Jesus who gives you strength.

Romans 8:37 you are more than conquerors through Him that love you.

Romans 8:31 you are told that if God is for you, it does not matter who is against you.

It is important to know who holds your future and your hand. Forget those things, which are behind you and keep reaching forward to those things, which are before you and put your life in the hands of the Man who calms the waters

~ 30 ~

> "God is your refuge and strength, a very present help in trouble."
>
> Psalm 46:1

৩৩৩৩৩৩৩৩৩৩৩

Our shortest walk in life is our walk into trouble. We try as much as possible to avoid it, steer around it, evade it, but it always finds its way into our path. At some point in your life, you will experience troubles, trials, and tribulations. These trouble times can be stressful, but it is also the gateway to discovering the power of God.

You can never truly understand God's power to deliver, if you have never experienced trouble. When God delivers you from troubles, it strengthens your relationship with Him.

God sometimes allows tests and storms in your lives, so you will get your attention and focus back on Him. God can bless you so much that you can start to "slack up" in spending quality time with Him. When troubles arise, it makes you realize that on your own, you cannot resolve these issues. But when your footsteps are ordered by the Lord, you know even though it seems impossible to you, with God all things are possible because you can do all things through Christ

Jesus who gives you your strength. There are even times when you seem to be where God wants you, and you still have troubles. Whether it is an act of God or an attack of Satan, God knows all about it and will fulfil His purpose. And as the saying goes, your troubles and trials do not come to tear you down, but they come to make you stronger in God.

Trouble is an asset that puts you in position to discover God's power in a personal way. God cannot answer a prayer, if it is not prayed. That is why He tells you in Psalms 50:15, "Call upon me in the day of trouble and I will deliver you and you shall glorify me." When you are in trouble, seek the face of the Lord, keep the lines of communication open with God and know that God is always with you, providing you with the resources needed to lead your life. Providing you with the strength to face tomorrow, no matter what tomorrow brings.

God said when you call on Him that He would answer. If there was enough power in God's answer to part The Red Sea in the day of Moses, to keep the sun from setting in the day of Joshua, to take the power from the flames in the day of the Hebrew boys and to shut the mouths of hungry lions in the day of Daniel, then surely God still has enough power in His answer when you call on Him in your day of trouble.

You may not be able to escape trouble, but you can have victory in the day of trouble. Do not become so consumed by troubles, trials, and tribulations that you fail to rejoice in them.

God is truly your refuge and your strength, a very present help in trouble. Though the earth be removed, though the waters thereof roar and are troubled, though the mountains shake with the swelling. Though the winds blow though the storm rage. In other words, though your bills are due, though there is trouble in the home, though they give you a hard time on the job, though they give you a hard time at the church, though there's sickness in your body, though someone has gotten on your last nerve. Stop your worries, stop your complaining, stop your doubting, stop your frowning, cease those fears and dry up those tears. God is right there to comfort you, to guide you, to hold you, to heal you and to deliver you.

~ 31 ~

"And be not conformed to this world: but be ye transformed by the renewing of your mind, that ye may prove what is that good, and acceptable, and perfect, will of God."

Romans 12:2

ഏഏഏഏഏഏഏഏഏഏഏ

When you wake up each morning, you have a choice to make. Just as you start your day choosing the food for your body, you also must choose the food your will feed your mind/inner person. As you are careful about your food choices for your physical body, you must take the same amount of caution when deciding which person, you will mentally feed. You can feed your spirit man, or you can feed your flesh. The one you feed the most will be the one to win. When you want something to grow you feed it and if you want something to die you starve it!

You get good at walking in the Spirit the same way you get good at walking in the flesh. Practice. The more you walk in the Spirit, the better at it you get. You may hit some wrong notes along the way, but the only way to get it right is to keep on walking in the Spirit. The more you pray, the easier it gets. The more you read the Word, the easier it gets to read the Word.

Walking in the flesh is the same way. If you keep at it, you can get good at it. It can become second nature so that walking in the Spirit seems abnormal and walking in the flesh seems normal. This is a tragedy for a Christian, to whom the flesh is legally crucified with Christ.

If you look in the mirror and don't like what you see, do something about it! Try changing your spiritual diet! There is a saying that goes, "garbage in, garbage out." Your heads can be like that; if you put garbage in, you'll get garbage out. But if you put the Word in and will get the Word out! Each day make an effort to sow what you want to reap! Sow good, reap good; sow bad, reap bad, the decision is yours.

As each new day presents itself to you, enter in with great expectation that God will do what He says. If you go in with no expectation, that is what you will get. Nothing. You serve a God who can take your ordinary day or year and turn it into an extraordinary day or year. It does not matter what may come your way, it's all about the attitude you have and having the faith that God will work it out in the way He sees fit for God always know what He is doing!

~ 32 ~

"I am Alpha and Omega, the beginning and the ending, saith the Lord, which is, and which was, and which is to come, the Almighty."

Revelation 1:8

※※※※※※※※※※※

There is a song that goes, "I rose this morning giving honor to the Father, honor to the Son, honor to the Holy Ghost." It would be so easy for me to talk about all the negative things in my life. But as I sit and think about Who God is, I am truly thankful to the songwriter for reminding you that it is because of Who He is that you should give Him glory.

So many times, you have tendencies to thank God for what He has done in your life. But how often do you just bask in thanking God for Who He is in your life? Just look at all the creation, the fish in the sea, the fowl in the air; the ants. Only God. Then look at nature and see how the flowers know when they are to bloom. The stars and the moon know they are to shine at night. Only God. The trees can grow up into some of the oddest shapes. The leaves on the trees know when to turn orange and when to turn green. Only God! Just look at the way man was formed and shaped into the image of God. You have use of your limbs, you have eyes to see, feet to walk, hands to clap, voice to talk. Now, who wouldn't serve a God like this! When you start thinking of Who God is – then you don't mind running when no one is chasing you; you don't mind crying when nothings bothering you; you don't mind shouting or clapping your hands. No, I don't mind at all. Because I know that it is in God that I live, move, and have my being (Acts 17:28). I can't do anything without Him. God is my Everything! He is my All in All! When I am weak, He makes me strong! When I have a hung down head, He is the Lifter of my head! When I am lonely, He is my Comforter! When I am in trouble, He is my Bridge over troubled water! When I am friendless, He is my Friend! When I can't fall asleep at night, He rocks me in the cradle of His loving arms! My God! My Peace! My Joy! My Song

~ 33 ~

"For God so loved the world, that he gave his only begotten Son, that whosoever believeth in him should not perish, but have everlasting life."

John 3:16

⊰⊰⊰⊰⊰⊰⊰⊰⊰⊰⊰

How many times have you asked someone, why do you love me? You often try to figure out what in your life merits the love of someone else. But have you ever just loved someone just because? No conditions, no strings attached, just because?

From the very beginning of time, you were on God's mind. Because God created you, everything that exists today was first originated in the mind of God. Before you were even formed, God loved you! While you were yet sinners, in your own state of rebellion against God, He sent His Son, who was without sin, to die for your sins so you could be brought back into a love relationship with Him. There is nothing in your life you can do to make God love you. God loves each of you, just because.

There is no why to His love for you. When you have a love with a why, it is conditional. You love because they love, or you love because they gave you the material things you so longed to have. God's love for you is unconditional. That is how your love should be. You were created in the very image of God and because He loves you unconditionally, and we should love others unconditionally.

Always know that there is One who loves you just because. As God is love, you too are love. You were made to receive God's love. In the same manner, you are to love Him in return just because. Not for the things He has blessed you with, but just love Him for Who He is.

~ 34 ~

"But the Lord said unto him, Go thy Way for he is a chosen vessel unto me, to bear my name before the Gentiles, and kings, and the children of Israel"

Acts 9:15

ഷ‍ഷ‍ഷ‍ഷ‍ഷ‍ഷ‍ഷ‍ഷ‍ഷ‍ഷ‍ഷ

There is no one on the face of the earth who lives an unusual life as that of the woman God would see fit to use for His glory and praise. If you are to be used by God, then you must be instruments prepared by the hand of God.

The woman God would see fit, by grace, to use for the blessing of others and the glory of Himself must know how to stand alone in the presence of God. Using this as time to meditate on God's word. Focusing on things above, not on things of this world. This may mean not following the crowd all the time. If you follow the crowd, you'll become like the crowd. If you follow the Savior, you'll become like the Savior.

For you to be used by God, you must be willing, burdened, and patient. Romans 1:1 reads "Paul, servant of Jesus, called as an apostle, separated unto the gospel of God." Here Paul is saying he is a servant of Jesus Christ. He is saying, "I am absolutely sold out to His will. I am willing to do whatever He tells me to do. I am willing to say whatever He tells me to say. I am willing to go wherever He leads me. I am a man who has made a choice. I am going to serve Him for all eternity." Jesus will not force you to do anything, you must be willing vessels, ready to work for God and do what He wants you to do. You are only usable to the degree that you are willing to surrender.

In being willing, you must also be real. Man looks on the outside. God looks at your heart. Ask yourself, why am I serving the Lord Jesus? If you don't love Him, if you haven't understood that nobody else will ever treat you like Jesus, then no wonder you are not being used of the Lord in the task He has assigned. A woman God can use is a one who is willing to say, "God, I just want what You want in my life."

Not only should you be willing, but you should have a burden for your fellowman. In Mark 10 you find that Jesus gives this as a rule in the Christian walk. Until you come to the place that you are willing to serve Him, you will never come to the place that you are willing to serve others. As you love Him you can start loving others. The way the people of the world are going to be won to Jesus is by Christians who are surrendered as servants to Christ, willing to serve others. You are willing to be used by God in your life and therefore, God can do something eternal through you.

You must also be patient. There are a lot of people in the church who want God's will for their life. But they cannot find it. It is because they have put a time table on God. They have said, "I have got plan B if you don't come through like I want you to come through." You find God's will for your lives when you are willing to accept it the way He does it and say, "God, whatever you want, I want. What do you want for me, Lord?"

Do you want to be used by the Lord? Do you really want to be used by God? If you want to be used, then decide. You can't serve two masters. Which one are you going to serve? How are you going to serve Him? Make a choice out of freedom. You've got to make a choice. Make up your mind. Are you going to serve Jesus or are you going to serve yourself?

You will never be used by God until you forsake yourself to Him. There is no in between ground.

~ 35 ~

"Let every thing that hath breath praise the LORD. Praise ye the LORD."

Psalm 150:6

ఆఆఆఆఆఆఆఆఆఆఆ

In life, you have heard about people talking about their many trials and tribulations and you may have witnessed your own. If you are among those who have never experienced any trials or tribulation in life, in the words of my grandfather, just keep on living. Just as sure as you live, at some point, you will all face trials.

Over the course of the years, I have lost many loved ones. Some losses have hurt a little harder than others, yet as I reflect I realize despite all the things I have gone through, the loved ones I have lost; my disappointments; blessings I have let slip away; times I lost my focus; possessions and battles I've lost, I did not lose my praise. Yes, it has been painful remembering some of the things of my past, but I praise God for bringing me through those times. I praise God for allowing me another chance to get things right in my life. I praise God for the memories I have of those whom have gone on before me. I praise God for my sanity in the midst of all the craziness surrounding me. I praise God for family and friends to help pray me through.

I still have hope, joy, faith and praise. I know the God I serve is an awesome God. It is He and continues to be He Who keeps me every day. There is nothing in my life I have done or can do to make me worthy of all the blessings He grants me, big and small. I owe God all my praise!

No matter what your situation may look like, I simply want to encourage you to never lose your praise. Just as in my case, the same holds true for you. The God you serve is an awesome God. It is He and continues to be He Who keeps you every day! There is nothing in your life you have done to make you worthy of the many blessings He grants you, big and small. You owe God all your praise!

Regardless of what you may lose along life's way, I encourage you to never lose your praise! Your God is indeed an Awesome God who reigns in heaven above with wisdom, power and love your God is an Awesome God who deserves your praise!